ANAMNESIS

By the same author:

The Mini Style Guide (2018)
The Beating Heart (2020)

ANAMNESIS

DENISE O'HAGAN

RECENT
WORK
PRESS

Anamnesis
Recent Work Press
Canberra, Australia

Copyright © Denise O'Hagan, 2022

ISBN: 9780645180886 (paperback)

A catalogue record for this
book is available from the
National Library of Australia

Cover image: 'Frax' by Kevin Dooley, 2015, reproduced under
Creative Commons Attribution 2.0 licence
Cover design: Recent Work Press
Set by Recent Work Press

recentworkpress.com

PH

To Darryl, Isaac and Dominic

Contents

*'An intimation of the Eternal
Return, or bitter-
sweet in the same cup, this draught
of absolute dark that shadow
-like we carry in us.'*

— David Malouf, *Towards Midnight*

*'And I will know what I am watching is
a passionate economy
we call the past. Although
its other name may be memory.'*

— Eavan Boland, *Watching Old Movies
When They Were New*

Subtext

I am talking of the dent in the hallway door,
The cracked halo of paint around the handle of
The third cupboard in the kitchen, the tracery
Of sentence scraps and childish doodles held
In the wax polish of an old oak dining table:
These things, the chipped and the stained,
The broken and the maimed, fill in pauses
In the official narrative of our daily lives.

Written into our walls and floors, inscribed
With incidental eloquence into the underbelly
Of our furniture, in gatherings of little lost items
Fallen into fluff behind sofas: here we may read
The subtext of our nights and days. We need to
Work backwards, build on the fretwork of fact
To feel the passion in a pressed flower falling
From the leaves of a novel, the heavy pull of
Domesticity in a torn-off shopping-list, touch
Grief folded into a curl of hair in an envelope.

Street seasons

Summer was marked out
In the red curve of watermelon slices,
Dripping water pearls from a tiered rack.

That russet-tinted after-season, autumn,
Blew in with the leaves, moist and cool:
By late afternoon, the pavements blushed.

Coiled in the sweet Christmas smell
Of ember-warm, shell-cracking chestnuts,
Lay winter, in rough newspaper cones.

As the air quickened and buds thickened
Spring slipped in, like a half-smile,
And the watermelons grew plump.

Love was almond shaped

Love was almond shaped
On sultry summer afternoons
When we sat outside in slatted light
With geraniums and the last of the washing
High above the eternal traffic noise
And other muted noise of the Eternal City
As she taught me how to crack them open,
Holding both my hands in one of hers,
Steadying my palm, spanning my fingers
Across the stern metal jowls of the nutcracker;
I'd squeeze and squeeze until each pitted casing
Strained and split at last, a rough unveiling,
And I, the beneficiary of sleek, sweet-tasting pods
Caught a blur of hair as she bent to scoop up splinters,
Her wedding band twinkling gold,
My whole world ringed by that balcony.

Hide-and-seek

St Peter's Square

The colonnade skirted the piazza
In a sturdy embrace, its squat base
Buttered by summer light. Edging back,
A girl could hide from her own mother
In there, watch the fumbling intimacy
Of a pair of early morning backpackers
And the slow progress of a nun
Fluttering across the grey paving.

Further back still, and the air was heavy
And cool. Thousands of years of secrets
Were folded behind those famous columns,
But all that would come later. For the moment,
It was a tall world slashed by shadow, hung over
By a pendant chain of lamps, and the click-clack
Of heels on stone as a voice urged her to hurry up
Or they'd miss the *casereccio*. Time enough
To cover her ears later when distance failed to
Reconcile the familiar columns of her childhood
With the most unholy of revelations.

Power cut

And when it happened, I'd feel my way
To the table in the hall, and slide open
The middle drawer, fingertips moving over
Keys and coins, pencil stubs—an assortment
Of things that no one wanted anywhere else—
Settling on a wedge of candles lying in wait
For precisely this occasion. For whatever may
Or may not have happened before or after,
A power cut forced an event.

In the ponderous moments it took our eyes
To realign themselves to abrupt non-light,
The air thickened from black to charcoal
Grey, until globes of lambent candle-light
Wavered in a different kind of warmth,
Painting us clownish and sudden strangers
To each other. I understood more about them
Then, in one moment of those waxen hours
When we burnt the wick of life, than
In the whole preceding week.

His fingers were square, blunt, not made
For the delicate strike of match to candle
And holding it steady. I remembered then,
His father was a farmer; for all the years
Of suits and ties and pencil-holding, these
Were farmer's hands. On the other side
Of me, beneath her silent, shadowed face
And the still curtain of her hair, my mother's

Polished nails were buffed by candle-light, as
She laid down her fork, pressed a napkin
To her lips. The dog nuzzled at my legs,
Somewhere a child cried, and here
A conversation was waiting to be had.

The almost-child

When she told me, I don't know. There was
A waft of fingertips at my hair, a kiss perhaps,
Her words, dredged up from the bog of the past—
                              I lost a baby
Two years before you were born. It was the word
Lost that stuck like Friday night's fishbone in my
Six-year-old throat. Surely my mother hadn't mis-
Placed my sibling-to-be within the safe shores
Of her own body? And yet—how relentless
Can a child's reasoning be!—you can't
Lose someone who'd never been there.

She'd had a heartbeat, then; she'd begun
Existing once, for a little while. She was a
Sliver of cells, a tadpole of budding organs,
Pressing towards definition. And then, something
Happened—a slip into oblivion, unfathomable and
Inexplicable. She never even had a name. She was
A shadow briefly cast, an echo reverberating, a
Ripple in time. She was an almost-child.

In among the ruins, love

After Cupid and Psyche, Ostia Antica, Rome

I tread the wide slabbed stone street, lined
With pines, thinking that those ancients knew
How to build a road alright. Passing the half-
Shell of an amphitheatre, the grid lines of
Tenements, remains of shops of wheat and
Wine and other goods, some with deities still
Rubbled at their doors, I come at last to stand,
As we stood so many times before, on the
Pale tessellated floor where, raised clean
Among the mosaics and sunbaked bricks
They stand, twin torsos, pedestalled: Cupid,
Accidental victim of his mother's ploy, in a
Marbled embrace with Psyche, beauteous
And unwitting prompter of so much envy.

You used to bring me here, too fractious
A child to be constrained by an apartment.
Meet at the statuettes in twenty minutes!
You'd say, and off I'd run; what would I give
To turn back now to you. I no longer wonder
What happened to their legs or why their
Eyes are blank, but fancy I can still feel—
As I watch a lizard slowly cross Psyche's
Polished thigh—in among the ruins, love.

Treading carefully

Lu-ma-ca, es-car-got was how I knew them,
Three-syllabled slugs with shells and antennae;
I warmed to the sound of their names as much

As them. But 'snail' has quite another effect;
I loved it less, this glutinous gender-bending mollusc,
Sly hugger of the dark side of our terrace flowerpots

And the undersides of damp garden things, curled
In fallen autumn leaves or clumped into compost.
We see them, the mornings after rain, slinking

Their way across the pavement, up walls. I tread
Carefully, to avoid the sickening crunch of shell
Underfoot, the gulping back of guilt. All things

Considered, they've had bad press: dismissed as
Pests, disdained for being slothful—a symbolism
Foisted on them in haste—at best, they're routinely

Transmogrified into a delicacy of buttered up and
Garlicked steaming shells in wine to feed another
Deadly sin—our drift to gluttony. Small wonder

They move slowly, carrying the weight of judgment
Coiled heavy on their backs. But how many of us know
That snails respond to having their shells caressed?

On getting my first glasses at thirteen

I had stretched the moment out so long, that I was
Irked it had finally come to this. After all, if I sat

At the very front of class and squinted, I could still
Separate most letters in each fuzzy clump of words;

My mind had grown efficient at filling in the gaps,
Thrilling at the revelatory moment willed by every

Calculated guess. I knew I couldn't see what others
Saw, but played it for a game. In a board marked out by

Adult rules, mine had an extra twist, a hidden handicap—
To fool the others I was just like them, to outwit friends

And teachers alike. I'd been doing so well until that day,
Waiting at a bus-stop with my mother, she read its number

Where I could barely see the bus; years of self-delusion
Fell from me in seconds, like tissue from a gift. I sensed

An appointment in the city, a day off school, and dared
To wonder what colour my frames might be. But later,

When the alien weight of my glasses was eased onto the
Bridge of my expectant nose, the world that was gifted me

Was one I no longer knew. Over the coiffed, puffed hair
Of the clientele, past the dull glint of tramlines, I blinked

At the ragged line of pine trees, their tapestry of needles
Pinpricked by daylight, and the brown curve of cones—

But also at my erratic complexion in the mirror, and its
Cool assessment in the optician's brooding eyes. Quickly,

I looked out again to see my father vanish round a corner,
Shadowed by the flutter of a floral skirt too close; saw

Fatigue powdered pinkly into my mother's cheeks; and for
A moment wanted nothing more with this sharp new world

Of clear-cut edges and definitions, this merciless laser vision
Against which human frailty stood not a chance. I folded up

My brand-new glasses, laid them in their brand-new case
Like a child's body in a casket, and stood up to leave.

The icon in Room 711

It was no good. My fledgling response
Stood barely a chance, its wings clipped in advance
By over five hundred years of analysis.

So there I stood in front of her, at last,
Trying, with all of my twenty-two years, to divest myself
Of the weight of her reputation, to take in the mystery of her:

So small, so dark. Was it disappointment I felt,
Beneath the clicking of cameras and the shuffling of feet
Of a greedy congregation intent on their passage

To the icon in Room 711? I avoided her eyes, settled instead
On the shadowy in-betweens of her fingers, the fine folds of fabric
Encasing her arms, the veil resting like gauze on her parting,

And watched, watched the effect of her happen—
This Florentine housewife, Our Lady of Perpetual Mystery,
Lassoing the crowd, through bullet proof glass, with that look,

And felt my reactions slipping into the mould, cooling,
Solidifying. So this is how it happens. And later, when we
Sift away the much touted facts of her journey to France,

And the court of a king, her sojourn in Napoleon's bedroom,
Her theft and unfillable two-year absence, in her layered existence
Between the light and the dark, there's still something else that remains.

The papering of distance

I picked out an old letter the other day
At random, from a drawer of old letters,
Ink-stained and fringed in red and blue,
The base of a coffee cup ghosting its corner,
And tasted again the flavour of a childhood
Spent drifting the slow space between things,
And glossy moments fashioned from nothing,
Kicking pebbles along a road to nowhere,
People-watching through grimy bus windows,
Or catching the bounce of the letterbox lid
In the fly-buzzing heat of an August morning.

Later, the careful unsticking of envelopes
From the mysterious other side of the world;
Smoothing out a latticework of handwritings,
The cursive, the slanted, the doodles and smudges,
Each one its own signature. All this a prelude to
The papering of distance lined in hopes and regrets
From aunts or cousins I could barely remember,
Or friends emigrated to their 'country of origin',
And in a postscript, how they yearned to be back,
While I, teasing stamps from envelope corners
In bowls of warm water, yearned to be there.

Afterglow

Children of foreigners in a foreign land, we grew up
In the afterglow of our parents' accidental stay. Work
Had offered them a validation and for us, by neat
Extension, a reason for our being there. Yet—

That we would one day leave was a given, surely as
The ancient walls hugged the still more ancient city,
Chemistry class fell on Monday afternoons, and it
Always rained at Easter. And so we became adept at

The skill of leaving or, put another way, the dubious art of
Non-attachment. We were the ones at home in alien queues
At airports, young veterans of the transit lounge, yet
Near strangers in our own countries, and ever alert at

Passport control. *Yes, I'm from here. No, I've never lived
Here. I'm just visiting.* The fissures chiselled deep into
The woodwork of our childhoods cracked wide open in
Adolescence. Far-flung offspring of expat privilege,

How many of us will admit to failure? Far easier
To view your life through others' lenses, agree that
Weren't we lucky to live like that, with *all that travelling
And such experiences*! But the deep-rooted knowledge

That you could cut yourself on sharp-edged dispensation,
Stagger in a shifting world of silhouettes and shadows,
And scramble to mimic the solid shape of other people's
Lives—this, we tend to keep to ourselves.

The house remembers

When its men and women had long moved on,
The strips of salted eggplant draining at the sink
That day, the ashen cluster of garlic cloves lying
On the kitchen bench waiting to be peeled and
Sliced. The scene was set, the pieces all in place.
But where was the woman? Why wasn't she there,
Hair pinned up, head inclined, chopping onions while
The oil heated, as she'd done so many times before?

The front door was ajar, her shoes were gone. Car keys
Glinted on the table in the foyer, the glass ashtray held
A single lipsticked stub. No breeze blew in, no curtains
Moved; the house held its breath. The year was 1963.
Down the hall, the children's beds were made, clothing
Folded neatly over the backs of chairs. Fluffy animals
At the pillows and windowsill, a stray button for an eye
Nestling by the bed leg on the floor: lone escapee.

But bathrooms were the giveaway, as the house knew well.
A sodden mass of tissues in the bin, a mirror pockmarked
In self-scrutiny, an unaccustomed disarray in the cosmetic
Drawer—the signs were there. And then—the spaniel in his
Basket raised his head, tail thumping at the click of heels
As the front door closed with fresh resolve. Now, lipstick
Would be reapplied, the blouse she'd bought the other day
Slipped on perhaps, wine and olives artfully arranged, but—

Would he notice? He was her world, and she was lost.
But she was back, and the house let out its breath.

Split ends and faded hopes

Eleven-forty on a Friday morning
And every chair is occupied, and some.
The muted rumble of passing traffic
Shudders the see-through salon door
As I idly wonder why it seems
Everyone is going somewhere else.

In this brief bubble of suspended time
We perch, cloaked and compliant,
Upright on our silver swivel chairs,
And pick up, with magpie alertness,
The covert stare of our mirror selves,
Stripped of artifice, their hopes and dreams
Spot-lit and framed by mock light-bulbs.

The hard tones of the small-time manager
Falter, as she murmurs *My son, he wouldn't
Have wanted me to let myself go*. And adjusts
Her glasses to take in the sparrow shoulders
Of a client being wheeled by, dabbing her
Newly tinted and puffed coiffure, because
I have to attend a funeral, you know, while
A teenager, in the drift between tint and wash,
Scrolls for messages that aren't there, trying not
To wonder *Will this make him love me more?*

In this sealed sliver of suburbia, heavy-aired
And intimate as a confessional, we offer up
Our confidences solemnly between frothy water
And waves of blown air, and feel our troubles
Dissolve in the listening, flushed away, as the
Tresses of our souls are massaged, conditioned
And rearranged by the quick, slick, skillful
Touch of the high priestess of style.

And so our split ends and faded hopes fall
Soft and silent to the vinyl floor, scooped
Up, nest-like, and swept out of existence,
Leaving our souls plumped up and glossier,
If only for a day.

My husband's grandfather, the jeweller

So we may find ourselves
Taking on other people's memories,
Slipping on the mantle of their lives
Until they become part of us
And walk where we walk,
Second-hand shadows,
Like the memory
Of my husband's memory,
When we went back,
Of that fastidious courteous man
Who dealt in heirlooms and timepieces
With an eye for the piece out of place,
So perhaps I was primed to be affected,
But anyway, when we pushed the glass door
Open, there we were face-to-face
With where he was no longer,
In black-and-crimson spot-lit décor,
And the practised smile of a well-heeled lady
Asking whether she could help us,
And while my husband, gesturing,
Was getting into a laborious explanation
Of the who and why and when
Of our presence,
I felt the clasp of the present loosen
And the facets of someone else's past
In a silent clamouring for attention
Press themselves in around us,

And gestured him in turn
To be silent and take in our surrounds:
The padded trays and cabinets of rings
And bangles, chains and chokers,
Of lockets and brooches and beads;
The sheen and the gleam
Of gold against cream
Amid gemstones on cushions of velvet,
And in my husband's eyes
A kind of desperation
Until I saw him see, off to the right,
The curl of the old wrought-iron staircase
Up to what used to be the working area
Where repairs used to be carried out—
How many used to be's—where
My husband's grandfather, the jeweller,
Used to work.

You've got his eyes
i.m. Patrick

You've got his eyes, she said.
And his smile, he added. They turned
To look at each other, their expression
One and the same. Literal minded
As we are at four or five, for a while
I considered myself a composite being,
A patchwork of pre-existing features,
Not an original, certainly not unique.

I was careful, later, with my own sons,
Not to bequeath them a cast of traits,
A sense their aptitudes and by extension
Their paths in life were preordained,
Determined by genetics.

And then one day, one cicada singing
Summer afternoon, reaching for distraction in
An old photo album, we opened at my uncle
In shirt and crooked tie, his shy half-smile
Lighting up the page. My youngest stared,
Then looked up at me, and said, 'Mum,
You've got his eyes.' I nodded and thought
Of my mother, the echoes and reverberations
She'd pick up in things and people
That others didn't see.

And my son, he had her mind.

Mother and child
Flesh and blood, 158.5 x 35 cm, 1997, artist unknown

She sat, like we all did, holding him wrapped in
Soft stripes of pastel pink and blue; you could tell
Those hospital blankets anywhere. The air was

Hushed around her, shadowed like the underbelly
Of a mushroom, painting her in the finest strokes of
Pale grey. I held my own complicated bundle of life

Tighter. Things were precarious, more than any of us
Wanted to admit. The nurses trod back and forth,
Watching us, and the clock; our half an hour was

Nearly up. She looked at me then, her eyes dark bruises
Against the shock of her face, and drew her child to
Her breast, swollen with undrunk milk. The blanket

Slipped from miniature limbs, a plastic anklet. Silently,
She pulled the blanket back and shielded him with the
Full curve of her body, brushing his head with her lips.

She would not give up; she would fill the space left
By his unresponsiveness, and tend that which had
Grown between them during their nine short months:

A portrait of mother love, blocked out there in the ward
In its most elemental form, unyielding in the face of fact.
I recognised myself in her, and shivered; she was all of us.

If I could

If I could show you the gossamer lining of flowers,
Or the world held in the reflection of a raindrop
Poised on a leaf edge, bulbous with possibility;

If I could impart to you a tiny fraction
Of the shimmering strength of a single strand of spiderweb
Bobbled with dew, swaying in the early morning light;

If I could turn you to the latticework of leaves overhead
Dappling you with patterns cut from the sky,
A geometry of diamonds, fashioned from light;

If I could fold you in my arms, as when you were born,
Sweep away the paraphernalia of broken adolescence,
Of a life staked out in childish trinkets and hospital bracelets;

If I could reach your hand, and bitten-down fingernails,
Squeeze out the pain, the fluttering insecurities
And still the butterfly palpitation trapped in your chest;

If I could do all this and more, I would—or so I dream,
And sweep away the crumbs of bitterness, to touch at last
That space which lies at the slippery heart of grace.

Stages of wanting

I held you close to impart my strength to you
To later pull away. I folded up unused baby clothes
Under fluorescent lights and all the time, all I wanted was

For you to live. Days when things hung in the balance
Saw me indulge in mental acrobatics, driving
A hard bargain with God, who saw fit to let you

Stumble into adolescence. Hawk-eyed, I scanned your face
For tell-tale blue about your mouth, and supermarket aisles for
The best organic produce, waged a domestic war on chemicals,

Sugars, preservatives and other kitchen culprits, all the while
Wanting nothing more than for you to find your place at school,
Keep fatigue at bay, and build yourself a cast-iron set

Of defences against this unforgiving world of ours,
Not realising, though I have tripped up so many times
Myself, that it is in the falling that we learn to stand.

Is letting go, I wonder, the highest form of love, akin
To death? I brought you up for this, I schemed and strove
For this. And yet I cannot help but hold my breath, seeing

The fluid curve of lorikeets against a purple sky, the cat's
Easy conquest of a fence, as I hear the grunt and heave of you
Pulling weights upstairs, honing your physique through

Sheer pig-headed will. Poised on the cusp of leaving,
Yet still not fully fledged, you flex your own wings
For flight; and it comes to me that after all, it is perhaps

The children who nail a truth where adults flail and flounder.
The intellectual approach misfires, cool analysis reaches
Freezing point; even poetry staggers in the face of this.

Now all I want, as I feel the shining weight of space and time,
Is to learn another form of love, and return to you the words
That you once offered me: 'I'll always be in your world.'

Porcelain leaves, the cream and the green

I admit it,
I don't even like them,
just bought them on a whim,
my hand closing around each
creamy sliced-off stalk end with
its cool clasp of overlapping leaves,
the same pallid green as the porcelain
dress of the tight-waisted, white-bodiced,
bouquet-clasping, porcelain lady pirouetting
on my mother's mahogany dresser and which
we had to keep there, year after year, because
'she was a gift, and just imagine if …!' but these
leaves are more damp tissues than porcelain, pressed
in one over another, and I rinse them slowly, almost
tenderly, leaning over the kitchen sink as the steam
begins to rise, feeling a spray of ridges as fine as
the veins in the underside of my wrist as,
caught up in yet another school lunch,
I turn my hand and with a furtive flick
into a serviette, fold them away—
so what am I doing
now, serving up
Brussel sprouts
to my family?

In limbo

We can circle around the fact of it
And, like the gulls, swoop and swipe, and try
In vain to get the measure of it, but when it happens,
The inevitable yet holds the greater shock. The phone call
Came at 4.45 a.m.; I looked at the square of pale blue
Above the kitchen window, and thought:
The sky will never look the same.

That it was all over twenty years ago
Matters not at all; in the double-take of time,
It could be yesterday that we drew up outside
Hospital doors yawning their acceptance
Of people such as us. In looking down
The deepening corridor of years, I see
The space he left is still not emptied, but
Chafes against the string of incremental actions
And the littleness of life. Today I make real coffee,
Inhale the aroma of jet-black beans, stretch clingfilm
Tight over tuna-and-mayo lunchboxes. Then,
I crushed the plastic beaker from his hospital tray
In my unforgiving hand; he despised
Coffee in plastic cups.

On the other side of the world, a memorial mass
Was said for him, but it is we who are left behind,
Who are in limbo, adrift in the eternal present,
Scrambling to fill in time and compensate our losses,
Chalk up a character for ourselves, and all the while
Unhad conversations ghost the hall, the dining table,

With family intimacies that never happened, for my sons
Only know their grandfather through hearsay, old photos
And the litmus test of time.

Twenty-two years

since I last heard your voice, or saw you
step off the plane at 76, quite an age to emigrate,
newspaper in hand as my mother pushed the trolley,
aware you weren't quite the man you used to be,
unaware of what you brought by merely being there,
grasping your trusty cherry wood walking stick
shiny handled from all the years of grasping,
time enough to scrape a meeting with my son,
who grew up not knowing what he missed—
yet still that great grey slab of time keeps stretching,
getting no more distant for being more thinly stretched
week by year by decade, and now you're doubling back
two countries ago, tea-towel slung over your shoulder,
pouring a glass of red and flipping potatoes in olive oil,
steadying the fry-pan with the wobbly black handle
as I slice garlic and onion, and tear off a chunk of bread,
jamming it between my lips as my mother taught me
to shore up the watering in my eyes.

If you don't know

I found Ward 9A alright, orange line threading
The corridors to Room 3. From cradle to coffin
We are forever contained by numbers.

Her broken sparrow of a body, her whiplash tongue
Weren't going to make things easy. She'd never been one
To fall in line or follow rules, and wasn't starting now.
I watched the nurse, slim, trim and bangled, glance
At her watch, pull up a chair. She laid the questions out,
Evenly, like cutlery on the dining table, shiny with
Common sense, the full backing of a committee
And the surety of limitedness.

Adrift in the hospital sheets, she preserved her silence,
As a lifetime's distrust of the medical trade bolstered up
Her fighting instincts. I could see her polishing up in turn
Her grenades of words, preparing her remaining artillery
Against this ultimate indignity, then draw the final battleline.

'Now, let's try this last one, shall we?' The slow thrum
Of nails on pad merged with the continuous bleep of
The monitor; the drumbeat of war. There was silence
As each surveyed the other, the sense of tempers fraying,
A gauntlet about to be thrown. (A tiered trolley, plastic trays
Piled high with sealed lunches, paused behind the curtain.)

'Young lady,' my mother spoke at last, 'if you don't know
What year it is, I'm not going to tell you.'

Waiting

I reach for the comb, mindful of the drag of rounded teeth across skin as translucent as tracing paper. My hands are the latest in a long line of hands that have tended that hair, and here in this final frame I recall what I never knew, the soft movement of a small hairbrush over a baby's head. Now her hair is feathery and light again, and makes such an imperceptible impression on the skull beneath that the comb becomes nothing more than an instrument of delicate rearrangement. I'm pleased with my efforts: she wears her hair like a nightcap, draping down past the globe of her still plump ear lobe and over the play of ridges at her collarbone. A strand of her hair flares auburn for a moment, or is it a trick of the light? Her physical casing is receding before me, and I become aware of something else emerging; I know that in tending my mother I am tending her spirit. She is neat, patient, waiting. I wait with her.

In sallow candle-light

The wind was getting up as we set out.
Plastic bags ballooned down High Street,
Snaring lamp-posts and mobbing gutters

As the rain began to fall. Death shrinks us
Like a doll, and in the steely presence of it,
You feel gauche and graceless to even be

Alive. Casketed in her best clothes,
Stilled and scarfed and lipsticked, with
Fingers threaded through with beads—

Was this her at all? She'd been made up,
Of course; the parchment line between
Skin and skull was tangible in sallow

Candle-light, the pale rounds of her eye-
Lids shone like bone, but the unthrobbing
Vein at her temple gave it all away.

Still the rain kept falling

I'll not forget
The sombre shuffle in
From the rain, the pain of it,
Of nods and handshakes,
Murmured condolences which
Cannot help but miss the mark
But it's all we have:
Inadequacy on a pedestal.

> *Oh, get on with it! She'd chuckle,*
> *Cross her legs and light another cigarette*

And so we did,
With the inevitable mini rituals
Attendant on the outward one:
The squeak of shoes on stone
And clearing of throats, misting of eyes
At the wavering brush of candle-light
And spray of lilies over her.

> *The moment's happened, then, she'd say,*
> *The one we shrink from, and push away until we can't*

Yet there's no end to what we can't admit
As later anecdote and wishful thinking
Shape our memory and, chameleon-like,
It changes in the telling. But this much I know:
Her dark-haired grandson who sat apart,
Inclined, black-shirted, at the piano, his
Fingers danced a song of his own making

Tenderly, as if he'd spent his short life
In preparation of this moment under
The thirteenth Station of the Cross.

She adored her music,
From Bach and Billy Joel to Casablanca*'s theme*

She was a good listener.
But now it was our turn to
Hang onto words, to incantations
Expressing the inexpressible.
I clutched my tissues, hot and damp
And still the rain kept falling.

In her letters, notes and diaries—a litany of ruminations,
Words had stretched her past her troubles, far beyond

The black bug of the waiting hearse
Was shiny, doors open, mouthing glassily
In the pale air, reflection-laden, gleaming,
As holy water splashed, like slivered
Tears on wood.

Contrary, contemplative, and one of a kind—
Mistress of the mercurial: my mother

The grave-studded hillside stretched,
Like a thousand-piece chess-set
With exhausted pawns, falling
And tilting Kings and Queens
Watching, as she disappeared
Under scoop after scoop of earth
The richer now for holding her.

Re-calling Sarah

I'm moved to write to you, whom I have never
known, and whom I have always known, though
you died long before I was born, and lived half

a world away. I look at my creased, handed-
down photo of your softly sepia'd twenty-year-
old self, and wonder. Your dark-eyed composure

composes in turn my thoughts; there's poise in
your posture, challenge in the tilt of your head,
a delicate sense of expectancy as you look back

through me and beyond, towards a future that
never really happened. The parameters of disease
marked out in the white-sheeted hospital bed,

the tread of nurses, the clink of medicine bottles
and their hopeless ministrations—all this a mere
decade away. For now though, you're all dressed up,

bride-like again, and oh, so elegant—a photograph
was, after all, no small occasion. But in your eyes
(my father's eyes, my eyes) is a foreshadowing of

a space where a life should have been. When you
coughed strawberry splashes through your hand-
kerchief, and sweated the night away, awakening

fatigued and heavy-lunged, they knew. You wept, as
they drove you away, the corridors of your memory
running you back to when you held your child's

heartbeat close to yours, and you were not covered
up, segregated, portioned off like something unclean.
And when they brought your son to visit, the nurses

bit their lips, and kept him at a distance; it was a
cruel farewell. I think he never stopped missing
you, and the missingness was passed down,

and down. So your photo still sits in front of me,
a haunting, present absence: you, whom I have
never known, and whom I have always known.

The longest journey

'Europeans who decided to make a new home in New Zealand embarked
on the longest journey of migration in human history.'
(Te Ara, Encyclopedia of NZ)

On 8 December 1864, the ship *Viola* set sail for New Zealand
with 348 passengers. It was one of the many ships carrying
immigrants from Ireland in the wake of the Famine.

We have great reason to thank God, who in
His Providence has placed us under the care of men

> Cramped into the tired, tiered bunks in steerage
> down below deck with the vermin and the seepage
> and the cargo and other government immigrants

not only well skilled in their several duties
as master and officers of the ... good ship V.

> pushing and shoving and jostling and squabbling,
> the filth was palpable, the stench near tangible
> and privacy was just a word

but also most anxious for the comfort
and well being of their fellows ...

> there, where tedium vied with fear,
> waves slapping and slopping the deck
> and froth dribbling like unmopped spittle,

she encountered contrary winds, which detained
her for ten days in the chops of the Channel,

and he wondered sometimes whether they'd make it
while his wife complained about washing in a teacup,
the potatoes and too-salty meat that never ran out.

Experiencing ... very unsteady and boisterous weather ...
rounded the meridian of the Cape of Good Hope.

'Hold your tongue, woman,' he told her.
'We're blessed to be here, and don't you forget it!'
She turned away from him then, and didn't turn back

Gentlemen, allow us to say ... that our ardent
and united prayers are that you may be spared

until the day their infant son coughed his life away
in her arms, and he gently prised his small body
away from the ship doctor's brandied breath,

to successfully pursue your highly onerous and useful
profession and believe that we shall ever remember

his rough farmer's hands shaking,
saw to it that he was wrapped in sackcloth
like the other little ones before him,

the very kind and generous treatment
that we have all on occasion received from you.

weighted and slipped overboard
with their muttered prayers and
gritted teeth and barely a splash.

The passengers ... all arrived in good health and there
were 8 births, and 12 deaths (11 infants and one adult).

Past and future tense

I see you look at the husk of me, and would have
Liked to let you know it's not what it appears,
And I don't want your pity. The weighing scales
Of body and soul are tipping now, working in
Inverse proportion. I gather up my days, feel the
Lip of time curl back on itself, washing away
My daily wearies, landing me on the shore of
Another place between a past that hasn't happened
Yet, and a future I know already. It's a coming home
Of sorts: every thought and feeling I've ever had, or
Might have had, or wished I hadn't—a nether world
Of possibilities, and future memories held in storage.

I could have done it better, sure, but—see? I put
Regret where it belongs, along with blame and
Grief and shame. I daisy-chain my smiles and
Tears, note the particular quality of the sky
At dusk, and admit again my shadow selves
I buried long ago with those I loved. Enough
Of such talk; it would mean as much to you
As Morse code would to me. Yet I see you
Discussing me, for I've become less a person
Than a predicament. Your words snowflake
The air; I sense the drift of your intent, and
Feel the white spaces of your pauses. I know
You know my circle's near-complete, but how
To intimate I'm far richer now than when

My soul was spread as thin as Marmite
In the heady rush of a full-blooded life?

A different kind of language

'All poetry, as discriminated from the various
paradigms of prosody, is prayer.'
— Samuel Beckett

I never bent my head to tread the short
Flight of stone steps down, carefully, or
Noticed that they were damply uneven,

Dipping in the middle. The silence and
Cool never closed their clammy arms
Around me, nor did my eyes adapt slowly

To take in the gloom. The single light-bulb,
Wire-looped from the peeling ceiling, and
Suspended in front of her raised portrait,

Never swayed before me. Yet technology
Proves an efficient conduit: I enlarge the photo
Little by little, notice more. On the low-slung

Vaulted ceiling, mould nests in the cracks;
Behind the plaster, the dull gleam of ancient
Limestone; variegated tiles line the floor,

Cracked, crooked. This is no heritage-listed,
Tourist-trodden city crypt, titillating visitors
With hidden tombs of unnamed saints; even the

Altar chair had lost its seat. And yet, and yet—
Reader, I could write this poem differently, seeing
This rank, dank place of poverty as begging the

Biggest question of all, and furnishing an answer
In a different kind of language. I could see in the
Punctilious cleanliness of the icon's plastic casing,

Not incongruity, but the distillation of infinity;
In the burning of the light-bulb, the stubborn
Glow of that which defies description, and lies

Beyond the daily realm of all we see and hear
And touch and taste, and symbolism's poor
Cousin, the known landscape of words.

Detritus

From the pages of Maigret, another mystery—half a
letter, *Dear J—*, a stranger's cursive folded familiarity

a set of heavy polished silverware, swaddled in crimson
velvet, when every meal-time was an ornate occasion

a glass jar of foreign coins, pocketed kings and queens
pressed up to heads of state, circular edges of situations

a recipe for a neighbour's cake for Easter (Sambuca
underlined) pencilled onto April in a calendar of 1974

a drawer full of the secret lives of diaries, scribblings
of years shared, mostly; the steady dribble of days

bus tickets, library stubs, postcards repurposed before
repurposing became the thing to do, mini bookmarks

a typewriter lugged from room to room, its vowels
fingertip-faded, and a carriage return that still sticks

a small vase of HB pencils, office biros, and a gold-
nibbed fountain pen, when writing was a physical act

a drawstring bag of black polish, brush and well-
oiled rags; even in the wheelchair, his shoes shone

and slipped down behind the filing cabinet, her
last X-ray, curved and shelved in its own dust.

I walk on seashells

I walk on seashells, I walk on oyster shells
And tread the fine-grained sand between,
Gaze at the rippling water's pearly sheen
Stretching to waterfront lawns of grand hotels,
The ebb and flow of the tide, the swells,
And wonder again what might have been.
For I lost it all, yet still I dream
Of castles, bells and citadels.
I gather my skirts, hold my head up high:
He bruised my body but not my mind,
My penurious family turned a blind eye,
Pray tell me, on whom could I rely?
My husband is seen as wealthy and kind—
But I'd rather the boarding house nearby!

Three instances

i

And I unwrapped
The tiny knitted woollen cap
And miniature booties fit for a
Doll, and laid them shyly over
A jumpsuit as soft a blue
As the skin around
My baby's lips.

ii

Stretched between generations
Like a washing line, youth cavorting
With the breeze on one side,
Age sagging the other, and me
In the middle, shielding my face
Against the pulse of life
With a basket of pegs.

iii

The couple on the seafront sat
On stick-like seats, still as the
Rocks above, bound by the space
Between them, any words ferried away
By the wind, and when I blinked,
There was only water lapping,
Rocks and sea, rocks
And sea.

The winds of our own desire

*The shade of Francesca da Rimini encounters Dante descending
into the second circle of Hell (L'Inferno, Canto V)*

Who is this, then, who dares to show his face,
What traffic has he with our fog and gloom,
The ceaseless moans of us deprived of grace?

Let him feel our agony, taste our doom:
We, whose chief sin was to succumb to love,
Are now condemned to this eternal tomb.

He pleads for my story, and like a dove
Borne on the soft wings of a summer breeze,
I drift down to him from the shades above.

Has he, perhaps, suffered the same disease,
The allure of love, its consuming flame?
Has his pride been singed in a wish to please?

Sharing our tragedy sharpens my shame:
For my husband's brother my passions flared,
Oblivious to risk and blind to blame.

It began with a love of legends shared
Which kindled in us yearnings most tender,
Though we knew if revealed we'd not be spared.

Oh, for those times of intimate splendour
Vanquished by a murderer's vengeful knife,
Whose rage forbade all hope of surrender.

Our poet may faint at this tale of strife!
We were granted what we sought to acquire;
Now we're joined forever, yet have no life.

What exquisite irony that we'll not tire
Of being lashed by the winds of our own desire.

Nature's grand chandelier

The yolk of the sun, by mid-afternoon
Lay heavy on us, to the shade we drew near,
Craving the night, the limpid light of the moon.

A child lifted her mask, asking, 'Will it end soon?'
Her mother replied, 'It's the usual, no need to fear
The yolk of the sun, by mid-afternoon.'

But the scent of the ash in the air at high noon
Wilted her will, made her want to disappear,
Craving the night, the limpid light of the moon.

'Where are you, my child?' Her cries, out of tune,
Died on her lips under nature's grand chandelier:
The yolk of the sun, by mid-afternoon.

The child stumbled on unseen, trying not to swoon,
Drawn to the shimmering sea, 'til there became here,
Craving the night, the limpid light of the moon.

Surrendering at dusk to a watery cocoon
She rejoiced, for she'd fled this smouldering sphere,
The yolk of the sun, by mid-afternoon,
Craving the night, the limpid light of the moon.

Rosedale, New Year's Eve

Batemans Bay, 31 December 2019

I saw my memories burn up
On the seven o'clock news last night
In a confluence of heat and wind,
Swept away in a wall of red.

In the thick, dirty-laundry light
Swathes of metal, dull as mustard
Lie draped like outsize sheets
Over an ashen ground.

The heavy silence stretches,
Hemming me in a world in waiting,
The kookaburra's cry a memory,
The goanna in the garden gone.

The corner of a protruding brick
Anchors me, in seconds, to my awkward
Ten-year-old self, apartment-reared,
Cramped by old-world ways.

Squinting in the early morning light,
Tentative in the face of so much space,
I slipped and stubbed my toe on a brick:
A sharp intake of breath decades ago.

Shards of childhood curl in on themselves
Huddling in corrugated contortions
And nestling between clumps of rubble
Like frightened puppies.

Politicians parry, prance and pirouette
Walking the tightrope of their ambition,
Clownish in their ineptitude:
No one's taken in any more.

The bush burns, the tide turns
And the world holds its breath.

A world in waiting

It's far safer now to step out alone
Into the legislated solitude of the night,

Yet the paradox lies heavy on you,
Practised recluse: you need to get out.

So you pull on your trainers, don your mask,
And slope off into the world of shadows.

*

Thick-trunked trees line the street, like lumpen sentinels,
Foliage swaying under ragged cones of yellow lamplight.

You catch the black-ribbed velvet curve of passing wings,
Heavy with connotation, in a pulse of air;

Hear the rapid padding of possum feet along a fence
In a fetid-sweet mound of damp, unraked leaves

By an uncollected rubbish bin; and notice, up above, a rat
Silhouetted astride a telegraph wire: perfect poise.

A great cheese of a moon hangs low among the stars,
A hefty, orange-coloured cliché: celestial marvel, the equinox,

Washing over pale houses, like mismatched teeth
Recessed into the darkening gums of the pavements,

Their owners hounded indoors, obliged to front at last
The rippling ramifications of their self-indulgence

And ask if this may be their own doing, or undoing,
As Pandora prowls the empty streets of an empty city.

*

Closing the front door behind you softly, you feel
Questions thicken in the steady onset of witching hour.

There's a slow stealth to your movements now;
You stand a while, attuned to the breathing of the house,

And it's with something approaching wonder
That you realise you relish your new alone-ness.

Goldfish in a pandemic

Beached, they are, these big humans,
Flailing around their lounge as they
Check for updates, make another coffee
(they've given up giving sugar up), and
Feed me a little more; I do an extra circuit
Lest I grow fat on the crumbs of their
Discontent. Through my bowl, little
Amy's eyelashes are wet as she watches me
Watching her; we have an understanding.
The others are trying: her mother, in a latent
Artistic impulse, took to painting me—
On a T-shirt of all things! But the rest
May as well hold up a mirror as stare
At me; for behind this new attentiveness
In the mosaic of their shrunken lives,
I know they see *themselves* in me!

Duplicity

It began well. Loneliness took a back seat
In my new surrounds, my hastily appointed,
Pandemic-induced home-office where,
Bubbled away from the push and shove
Of city streets, the boredom of the boardroom,
My natural shyness ventured out, asserted itself;
Found solitude to its liking, demanded more.
In my new continuum, with the keyboard
My slim black portal to the outside world,
I cranked up the pace, accomplished what I had
To do in record time and, like a latent adolescent
Dizzied by the siren call of cyberspace, wallowed in
A myriad sites and groups, buffered by geography
And the knowledge I would likely never meet
The people behind the posts. There's relief in that.

Most of the time, I hold my duplicity at bay,
Quell the flaring of frustration that there's nothing
Between like and love, no way to say unsure,
Or give doubt due consideration. Yet in all this
I am complicit, and push away a foggy awareness
That a certain levelling out is taking place, that
I'm choking in the silken clutch of supposed
Communication. My coffee grows cold; so too
The irony that I've never had so many friends,
Yet have seen my neighbour only once.

El Alamein Fountain

You're the grande-dame of the Cross,
The liquid Medusa of a hundred stalks
Outwitting gravity and hooking stares:
Some call you a dandelion, or giant thistle.

Presiding at the junction of hope and despair,
Amid inner-city clamour and hard neon lights,
You tilt and you sway in your spray of a dress,
Winking as night falls, and drawing a crowd.

The Powerful Owl is
listed as vulnerable

This feathery-coated, creamy-collared
Yellow-eyed predator now finds himself,
If only he knew it, in an unprecedented
Situation: the Powerful Owl is listed as
Vulnerable. What match his slow blink,
His heavy winged progress in the dark
Hours before dawn, with the metallic wink
Of the imminent bulldozer; his vast wing-
Span and perilous claws with the bloated
Ambitions of local government?

But the future won't happen for a little
While yet. Still he nests high in the
Hidden hollows of ancient eucalypts,
And still he cries as he glides the night,
Staking out his territory before roosting
Season as Council prepares to *revolutionise*
The movement of humans across the city,
And gash the gully for a tunnel. For while
It is an *offence to harm a protected animal,*
Their habitat, though a designated
Wildlife protection area, would seem
Fair game for all. Ironies nestle
In the ways of the law, and rhetoric
Has got the better of us: we can
Persuade ourselves of anything now.

An appetite for whimsy

The place writes herself, this
Wild slash of a gully, between
Ancient rocks in an ancient land,

Sequined in the silver falling
Of countless eucalypt leaves, as,
Awestruck on an ordinary, extra-

Ordinary day, we tread the path
By the sandstone rocks marking
The pulsing of her watery artery,

Hoping against hope for the
Flick of a fish or curl of an eel,
Or a rare glimpse of one of the

Small shy existences to which
Her slopes are still habitat—the
Superb Fairywren, the Sacred

Kingfisher or Bibron's Toadlet—
Incontrovertible proof that the
Human appetite for whimsy is

Undiminished by the imminent
Prospect of urban development,
And the possibility of extinction.

Worrying about the lorikeets

It'll never last, they said, with more
Than a hint of the oracular. He avoids
Garlic & olive oil, doesn't drink Shiraz;
Meat-and-three-veggies leave her cold.
He opts for Def Leppard to her Bach,
Harbours a suspicion of art galleries,
And riskiest of all, though she's a fan
Of the silver fern, she doesn't get the
Finer points, or indeed the point at all,
Of rugby. Yet for better or for worse,
The knot was tied; and were someone
To ask her later why it held, she would
Have shrugged, unsure of what to say.

But just the other day, walking past
A shudder of wings by the tree at the
Curb, he admitted to worrying about
The lorikeets, and what might occur
If their senses were to lag behind the
Wheels of a speeding car, though she
Laughed away such fears. But when,
On their return, he knelt down longer
Than he needed to over the emerald
Mound of still-warm feathered flesh,
She saw in his upturned eyes the weight
Of its dumb pain—then it was that she
Remembered what she'd always known.

Notes

About the title: The word 'anamnesis' comes from the Ancient Greek 'Aνάμνησις (anámnēsis), signifying a calling to mind of past events, or recollection. In the Platonic epistemological tradition, recollection was understood to mean the gradual uncovering of ideas already known by the soul, perhaps before birth. Knowledge, therefore, was seen as being innate and located inwards in the immortal soul rather than in the external world.

'In among the ruins, love': The ancient city of Ostia Antica had always been strategically important. Under the Emperor Claudius, it became the major harbour city of Ancient Rome, where the ships arrived carrying grain from the Empire's territories in Africa, which was then ferried to Rome. Originally situated at the mouth of the river Tiber (hence its name, from the Latin *ostium*, or 'mouth'), today it lies roughly 3 km east of the river mouth due to the effects of silting.

The statue referenced in this poem is located in the House of Cupid and Psyche at Ostia Antica. In classical mythology, Venus (Aphrodite, Gr.), mother of Cupid (Eros, Gr.), being jealous of the exceptional beauty of Psyche (soul, Gr.), instructed him to shoot a golden arrow into Psyche which would cause her to fall in love with whomever was in front of her; instead, while contemplating her, Cupid accidentally scratched himself with his own arrow, and was instantly and permanently smitten.

'The icon in Room 711': Arguably the world's most recognisable painting, the *Mona Lisa* (painted 1503–19), now resides permanently in the Louvre's Room 711, in the Salle des États. Leonardo's subtle use of *sfumato*, soft gradations of light and shadow, lend the sitter the air of mystery for which she is famous.

'The house remembers': Inspired by the American drama television series *Mad Men*, in particular its portrayal of women in the early 1960s.

'If I could': Ebstein's Anomaly, with which my son was born, is a rare congenital heart disease which involves the displacement and malformation of the tricuspid valve. In severe cases it may lead to a flow of blood into the right atrium, in turn causing the heart to become enlarged. It affects one in every 20,000 live births.

'Re-calling Sarah': In remembrance of my grandmother, who passed away from pulmonary tuberculosis in 1932 in Waikato Hospital, New Zealand, and was buried in the Old Cemetery, Te Kuiti. She was 32.

'The longest journey': This hybrid poem references one of the many perilous voyages made by immigrants escaping Famine-torn Ireland. Among those on board the New Zealand-bound *Viola* were my great great-grandparents, John and Bridget O'Hagan, and their sons, one of whom, eight-month-old Edward, died at sea. The ship docked in Auckland on 4 April 1865.

The poem is composed of selected extracts from transcripts of letters to the *Viola*'s Captain, Officers and doctor as well as an extract from the official report of the ship's arrival (*Southern Cross* newspaper, 22 and 29 April 1865, and 5 April 1865 respectively, reproduced by courtesy of the National Library of New Zealand). All quoted matter appears in italics, and is juxtaposed with adapted portions of my own poem 'Blessed to be here' (originally published in *The Beating Heart*, Ginninderra Press 2020).

'A different kind of language': Based on a photograph taken by my father of a small crypt in a church in the south of Italy, c. 1980. Despite, or perhaps because of, the state of its disrepair, he was struck by it, and I in turn was struck by his photograph of it.

A crypt, from the Latin *crypta* (vault), is a stone chamber under the floor in a church which often contains coffins or other religious relics. It may also contain an *altarino*, or little altar.

'Detritus': From the Latin *detritus* (n), from *deterere*, meaning 'a wearing away' (from *de-*, 'away', and *terere*, 'to rub or wear'). Figuratively, it is used to indicate debris, or waste material.

'I walk on seashells': A Petrarchan sonnet touching on one woman's spirited escape from domestic violence during the late nineteenth century, the solace she finds in freedom, and her ironic speculations while walking at the seafront. Such female 'runaways' were at great risk of ending up in brothels or institutions.

'The winds of our own desire': This *terza rima* sonnet is inspired by Canto V of Dante Alighieri's *Inferno*. Like the rest of the *Divine Comedy*, it is remarkable not only for being written in the vernacular, but also for its deep understanding of, and compassion for, human frailty. Its subject is Francesca da Rimini whose husband, on uncovering her affair with his brother Paolo, had stabbed them to death, and she finds herself condemned to spending eternity in the very state she had craved during her lifetime.

'Nature's grand chandelier': Written one afternoon in January 2020 when the sky appeared obliterated by a blanket of dust and the sun a sickly yellow, this is a villanelle in the time of climate change.

'Rosedale, New Year's Eve': My cousins' house at Batemans Bay was one of the many homes destroyed by the bushfires. It exploded on New Year's Eve, 2019.

'A world in waiting': A musing on one of the effects of lockdown in Sydney during the first wave of the Covid-19 pandemic.

'El Alamein Fountain': The heritage-listed El Alamein Fountain in Sydney's Kings Cross was built as a memorial to soldiers who died in 1942 in the battles at El Alamein, Egypt.

'The Powerful Owl is listed as vulnerable': The Powerful Owl (*Ninox strenua*) is Australia's largest owl, living in the forests and bushland of the east coast. It is the male who hunts and defends their territory, bringing food to the nesting female (hence the poem's use of the male gender).

As a predator of rodents, possums and small birds, it is a natural guardian of biodiversity.

The italicised words and phrases are quotes from the *Biodiversity Conservation Act (NSW) 2016 (No. 63)*; the NSW Government Beaches Link Willoughby fact sheet, Nov. 2019; and the *Companion Animals Act (NSW) 1998 (No. 87)* (under which Council declared Flat Rock Gully a 'wildlife protection area').

'An appetite for whimsy': Flat Rock Gully, on Sydney's lower north shore, was home to the Cammeraygal people some 5,850 years ago. Today the area is one of the city's main wildlife corridors, and key to maintaining biodiversity. The Western Harbour Tunnel and Beaches Link will split this corridor and destroy extensive bushland, the effects of which are potentially irreversible.

Acknowledgments

My sincere thanks to Shane Strange and the team at Recent Work Press for their invaluable work in helping nourish and promote the art of poetry. To have my collection included among their books is an honour.

In addition, I extend my deepest gratitude to my family and the warm circle of writers-turned-friends for their critical support of my work, whose presence has provided a much-needed balance to the necessarily solitary business of poetry-making: Dave Kavanagh, Jena Woodhouse, Anne Casey, Angela Costi, Felicia McCarthy, Audrey Molloy, Daragh Byrne, Moya Pacey and Mario Baghos.

Finally, I acknowledge the editors of the following publications in which versions of some of the poems in this book were originally published: *Bluepepper*; *Books Ireland*; *Brushstrokes II, Ros Spencer Poetry Contest Anthology 2020–21*; *Burrow*; *Empathy: 2018 Australian Catholic University Poetry Prize Anthology*; *FemAsia*; *fourW thirty-two, Booranga Writers' Centre Anthology 2021*; *Grieve: Stories and Poems of Grief and Loss* (Vols 8 and 9); *Hecate*; *Legacies: South Coast Writers Centre Anthology, 2021*; *Live Encounters Poetry & Writing* (11th Anniversary Edition, Vol. 1); *Lothlorien Poetry Journal*; *Meniscus*; *Mingled Voices 6, International Proverse Poetry Prize Anthology 2021*; *Not Very Quiet* (Issue 7); *Quadrant*; *Resilience: 2021 Australian Catholic University Poetry Prize Anthology*; *Sutherland Shire Literary Competition 2020* (magazine); *Tarot* (Issue 1); *The Copperfield Review Quarterly*; and *Vox Galvia*.

The following poems were awarded or recognised in literary competitions:

'Love was almond shaped' won the Dalkey Poetry Prize, 2020 (Ireland) and was Highly Commended in the Francis Ledwidge International Poetry Award, 2020 (Ireland).

'If I could' won Second Prize in the South Coast Writers Centre Poetry Award, 2021 (Australia).

'Still the rain kept falling' won Second Prize in the Sutherland Shire Literary Competition, 2020 (Australia) and was nominated for Best of the Net, 2020.

'In limbo' won Third Prize in the International Proverse Poetry Prize, 2021 (Hong Kong).

'Mother and child' was Highly Commended in the Goldsmith International Poetry Competition, 2021 (Ireland).

'Re-calling Sarah' was Commended in the ACU Poetry Prize, 2018 (Australia).

'My husband's grandfather, the jeweller' was Commended in the Woorilla Poetry Prize, 2020 (Australia).

'Stages of wanting' was shortlisted in the ACU Poetry Prize, 2021 (Australia).

'Street seasons' was longlisted in the Segora International Poetry Competition, 2020 (France).

'Past and future tense' was selected to be read at the Spirit of Renewal Festival, 2021 (Sydney).

About the author

Denise O'Hagan was born in Rome and lives in Sydney. She has a background in commercial book publishing in London and Sydney, and worked as an editor for Collins, Routledge and Cambridge University Press, and was consulting editor for the State Library of NSW. In 2015 she set up her own imprint, Black Quill Press, through which she assists authors wishing to publish independently. Her late mother's novel, *Jerome & His Women*, which she restructured and copy edited, was shortlisted for the Institute of Professional Editors' inaugural Rosanne Fitzgibbon Editorial Award, the 'Rosie' (2015).

She is the author of *The Mini Style Guide* (Black Quill Press 2018) and *The Beating Heart* (Ginninderra Press 2020), editor of *Chinese Whispers: In Search of Ivy* (Black Quill Press 2018), *A Roman Death* (Black Quill Press 2017) and *Jerome & His Women* (Black Quill Press 2015), and co-editor of poetry anthologies *Messages from the Embers* (Black Quill Press 2020) and *Poetry for the Planet* (Litoria Press 2021). She was also Poetry Editor for Irish literary journal *The Blue Nib* (2019–2020) and guest editor for *Live Encounters*, 'Special edition featuring poets from Australia & New Zealand Aotearoa' (May 2021).

Her poetry has been internationally published and awarded, and includes recognition in the Dalkey Poetry Prize (first prize), the Adelaide Plains Poetry Competition (first prize), the South Coast Writers Centre Poetry Award (second prize), the Sutherland Shire Literary Competition (second prize), the Proverse International Poetry Prize (third prize), the Stephen A DiBiase Poetry Contest (finalist), the Francis Ledwidge International Poetry Award (high commendation), the Goldsmith International Poetry Competition (high commendation), the Scribes Writers 'Poetic Licence' Literary Award (high commendation), Australian Catholic University Poetry Prize (commendation and shortlisting), the Woorilla Poetry Prize (commendation), the Saolta Arts Poetry Competition (shortlisting), the Booranga Literary Prizes (shortlisting), the Women Writers National Writing Competition (shortlisting) and the Robert Graves Poetry Prize (shortlisting).

The publications in which her poetry appears include *Books Ireland, The Ekphrastic Review, New Reader Magazine, The Copperfield Review Quarterly, The Enchanting Verses Literary Review, Miletus International Literature Magazine, Scarlet Leaf Review, Eureka Street, Other Terrain Journal, Not Very Quiet* and *Australian Poetry Collaboration.* Her poems have also been translated into Spanish and published in *Cardenal Revista Literaria* (Mexico) and *Revista Poesía* (Venezuela).

This is her second collection of poetry.

Website: https://denise-ohagan.com/

www.ingramcontent.com/pod-product-compliance
Ingram Content Group Australia Pty Ltd
76 Discovery Rd, Dandenong South VIC 3175, AU
AUHW020721050325
407891AU00005B/30